Free Your "NO"

100 Reasons to Say "No"

End Exhaustion, Gain Clarity, & Create Space

by

Dr. Timogi

Published by
Create & Facilitate, LLC
www.CreateAndFacilitate.com
Printed in the United States of America

Contents

INTRODUCTION 1

THE SACREDNESS OF "NO" 9

THE COST OF YES 15

THE WEIGHT OF YES 21

"NO" COMMANDS RESPECT 27

THE RELATIONAL "NO" 33

"NO" PROTECTS 39

"NO" REDIRECTS 45

"NO" HEALS 51

"NO" SURVIVES 57

"NO" IS STRATEGIC 63

"NO" IS HUMANE 69

"NO" FORECASTS 75

"NO" GROWS AND ABOUNDS 82

"NO" BUILDS ROOTS 88

"NO" IS AN ADULT 94

THE CLARITY OF "NO" 100

"NO" BINDS AND SECURES 106

"NO" DISCERNS 112

"NO" IS CAPTIVATING 117

THE JOY OF "NO" 123

CONCLUSION 129

ABOUT THE AUTHOR 143

INTRODUCTION

Free Your "No."

"No" is two years old.

A two-year-old is one of the most powerful beings on the planet. How? With a single word: "No." At that age, they learn it, wield it, and repeat it with unapologetic boldness. Parents call it the terrible twos, but what if it isn't terrible at all? What if it is simply power discovered too early to be managed?

That tiny voice screaming "No!" is really making a declaration of independence, enforcing boundaries, and exercising keen self-awareness. It's both a refusal and a demand.

Somewhere along the way, though, we outgrow our boldness. We learn to please, to soften, to say yes even when our spirit is screaming no. This book is about reclaiming that lost power. Like that fearless toddler, we, too, must learn to embrace the freedom, clarity, and authority found in the word "No" because sometimes the most powerful way forward begins with refusal.

Free your "No."

You get a "No," and you get a "No," and you get a "No!"

This is not a book about becoming difficult, heartless, or selfish. It's not a manual for dodging responsibility, ghosting people, or shutting out love. It's not permission to be rude, reckless, or careless with others. This is not about saying no to everything; it's about saying no to the wrong things so you can say yes to the right things. Complaining is easy. Struggling is common. But standing in your power, that's rare. That's what a toddler does, and that's what this book is about. Not excuses but strength. Not retreat but authority. This book is not about saying no to everything.

Free your "No."

Abra Cadabra, "NO!"

Do not believe that once you say "No," your life magically clears space for every dream and goal. Life does not work like that. There will be times when your "No" comes with sacrifice.

There will be times when you give the hard "No" or the reluctant "No" to something even when your heart whispers "Yes." There are many kinds of "No." The tough-love "No," the I don't feel like it "No," the protective "No," the boundary-setting "No," the self-care "No," and the wisdom "No." Each one has power, not magic.

Free your "No."

Is it "No" Time?

This book is here to help you identify those moments where your "No" is meant to be free, so you can release it without guilt, without apology, and with the clarity that your yes will always mean more when it's anchored by the right "No."

Free your ability to advocate for yourself. Walk in agency so powerful it does not people-please, succumb to peer-pressure, or cower at difficult decisions.

Free your "No."

Free Your "No."

"No" as hope.

This book is hope for anyone who has ever struggled to say "No." If you've ever said yes out of guilt, fear, obligation, or the desire to please, this book is for you.

If you've felt drained, overlooked, or resentful because your yes cost too much time, energy, and resources, this book is for you. Here you will find the words, the courage, and the clarity to speak your "No" without shame.

Hope lives in the realization that "No" is not rejection; it is direction. "No" is not harsh; it is healing. For this read and importance, I've intentionally emphasized "No" with uppercase and

Free Your "No."

quotes, while yes is not. It serves as your reminder that freedom begins with the powerful word "No."

Free your "No."

THE SACREDNESS OF "NO"

9

Free Your "No."

"No" is sacred.

Saying "No." is sacred. It declares that not everything and everyone can have access to you. When you say "No" you declare yourself whole, unavailable for reckless consumption. "No" releases a divine boundary that guards your life, your energy, and your purpose. You are not all things to all people, and you were never meant to be. "No" preserves your wholeness, your clarity, and your freedom. "No" is not about limitation but liberation. It is the altar where clarity is kept, the sanctuary where peace is preserved. Speak! Say "No," because it is, and will always be, sacred.

Free your "No."

"No" is a basic human right.

Declaring "No" is a basic human right. Just like breathing, eating, and resting, the ability to say "No" is essential to survival. Yet too often, we've been taught to feel guilty for using it, as if protecting ourselves requires permission. It is a declaration of self-respect, a boundary setting word that protects your time, energy, and humanity. To strip someone of their "No" is to strip them of their freedom as a human being.

Free your "No."

You don't need a good reason to say "No."

That's right, ladies and gentlemen, we've been taught and conditioned to believe that every "No" requires an explanation, a justification, or a "good" reason. We've been made to think we must qualify our refusal to make it acceptable. The truth is simple: "No" doesn't need an explanation, a qualifier, or an apology. You have the right to say "No" without any reason at all, simply because you don't want to.

Free your "No."

"No" needs no translation.

Travel the world and say this small, two-letter, simple word and people will understand you. "No." It is one of those words that is the same in multiple languages. Even many of its variations are similar, Portuguese; não, Romanian; nu, Dutch; nee. That is the power, strength, necessity and authority in the word "No."

Free your "No."

Free Your "No."

"No" is the honest answer, anyway.

There are many quotes, phrases, and anecdotes centered around truth. There are religious texts that explore the concept of truth and its power to liberate. If your thoughts, your heart, and even your body all tell you "No," trust that wisdom. That "No" is not only the genuine and honest answer – it's the kindest gift you can give to your soul.

Free your "No."

THE COST OF YES

15

Free Your "NO"

Yes, is a thief of purpose.

The frivolous yes is robbing you of your purpose. You're out here spending time and energy on things you don't even want to do. That's the part you won't say out loud. Deep down, you know most of those yeses weren't given from a place of desire or purpose. They were guilt, pressure, or fear in disguise. The truth? Your purpose lives on the other side of your "No." Every time you use it, you carve a path back to yourself. So, stop hiding it, use it.

Free your "No."

Without "No," yes has no worth.

A person who says yes to everything cheapens their yes. When you say yes too often, your yes stops carrying weight. It becomes a doormat, the place where everyone wipes off the dirt, grass, mud, gum, and residue they've picked up from the streets of life. Instead of being honored, your yes gets trampled, used up, and taken for granted. Common. Average. Basic. And when your yes becomes so freely given, people stop seeing you as valuable.

Free your "No."

The wrong yes produces instant regret.

Regret carries sadness and disappointment, almost a repentance over a missed or lost opportunity. When you say yes to something that should have been a "No," that regret shows up almost immediately. The heaviness, the sorrow, the disappointment, all of it floods in because you betrayed yourself. But you don't have to carry that weight. You can avoid it altogether by doing something simple, yet profound. Say "No."

Free your "No."

A guilty yes is a cowardly "No."

When you feel guilty about your yes, then "No" was the correct answer all along. When your yes comes with shame, regret, and turmoil, it was simply a cowardly yes that should have been a "No." So put your grown-up pants on, shoulders up, stand up straight, get flat-footed, and give a powerful and meaningful "No" over a cowardly yes.

Free your "No."

Free Your "No."

A dirty yes binds.

Feeling stressed, trapped, anxious, or bound because you gave out a dirty yes? A dirty yes is knowing that you wanted to say "No" but said yes instead. Perhaps you even knew beforehand that the person was going to ask you for something, you knew you didn't want to do it, but you said yes anyway. A dirty yes is born out of a condition or an obligation to someone or something to which you are not obligated. A dirty yes is sometimes fueled by pride or self-promotion. That's why you feel stuck, captive, caged up, bound, and imprisoned by your yes.

Free your "No."

THE WEIGHT OF YES

21

Free Your "NO"

Today's "No" prevents tomorrow's resentment.

There's a deep, aching resentment that grows when you say yes when you should have said "No." The moment you give that yes away, the weight of resentment takes over. Now you're stuck wrestling with the mental battle and heartache that could have been avoided if you had honored your "No." The person who received your yes is sleeping peacefully tonight, but you're the one tossing and turning, restless and resentful. That's the hidden cost of silencing your "No."

Free your "No."

Yes without "No" will bury you.

A constant stream of yeses piles up like dirt, covering your joy, your energy, and eventually your identity. Every time you say yes when you should have said "No," you get buried beneath another shovel of dirt, and you're exhausted, overwhelmed, and unrecognizable. A buried life is not an abundant life. Your "No" is the shovel that digs you out, the boundary that keeps you breathing, and the way you get out of that hole until you reach the sun.

Free your "No."

Yes without "No" erases you.

Every time you agree out of guilt, fear, or pressure, you carve away at your identity. Piece by piece, your voice fades, your desires dim, and your presence shrinks. You become a shadow, seen but no longer in your wholeness. Erasure doesn't happen all at once; it's the slow surrender of self until you are busy but invisible, active but absent, loved but not known. When yes and "No" walk together, your essence remains intact. You stay present, powerful, and visible, reminding the world that you are here.

Free your "No."

Yes without "No" empties you.

Each careless yes pours out a piece of your strength, leaving you drained, depleted, and disconnected from yourself. You cannot keep giving without refilling, and you cannot refill without boundaries. A constant yes is a slow leak, silent but deadly, until you wake up empty. But when you add the power of "No," you stop the leak. You hold on to your energy, your joy, and your identity. "No" makes your yes sustainable, meaningful, and life-giving.

Free your "No."

Yes without "No" silences you.

Shhhhhhhh. Do you hear that? It's an eerie kind of quiet. Don't mistake it for peace, it's absence. It's your absence. The sound of your own desires fades until they are whispers you can barely recognize as your own voice. Each forced yes hands pieces of your voice to others, until you're speaking, but it's not really you or on your own behalf. It is their agenda, their script, their demands echoing through your mouth. That is the theft of voice. You're seen but not heard. "No" breaks the silence and releases your sound.

Free your "No."

"NO" COMMANDS RESPECT

27

Free Your "No."

"No" is a symbol of respect.

Someone who says "No" distinctly and matter-of-factly is saying "I respect myself, I respect my time, I respect my voice, I respect my opinion, and I respect my ability to look you in the face and say "No." I won't hesitate with empty words like "let me think about it," or my favorite, "let me pray about it." And when you learn to respect your own "No," those who love you, value you, and care about you will respect you for your "No."

Free your "No."

"No" teaches others how to treat you.

Every time you say it, you set the standard for how people engage with you. Boundaries aren't built by accident; they are taught, moment by moment. If you always say yes, people learn to expect your time, your energy, and your presence on demand. But when you stand on your "No," you send a clear message: My worth has limits, my space matters, and I will not be mismanaged or abused.

Free your "No."

"No" defines the sacrifice.

Making sacrifices is necessary in many areas of life. Sacrifice can be noble, rooted in principle, and grounded in meaning. That's where strength is found, so you say yes. But sacrifices can also be performative, done for praise, recognition, or to keep up appearances. If that's the real reason you said yes, it's time to pause, get honest, and maybe even get some therapy, but here is where you say "No."

Free your "No."

"No" is proof you are not disposable.

Disposable things are used up, tossed aside, and forgotten. You are not that. When you say "No," you are announcing that your existence cannot be reduced to tasks, favors, or constant availability. You are not here to be consumed until empty. You are here to be valued, respected, and seen in your fullness. "No" is the voice of your dignity, declaring I am not here to be used. I am here to be honored.

Free your "No."

Each "No" conserves your power.

Do you want more power in your life? The power to create joy. The power to heal. The power to build peace in a clutter-free space. The power to prioritize what matters. The power to learn something new. The list goes on and on. The power you crave is already yours. It's just being drained. Every unnecessary yes takes energy from those areas. Every time you silence your "No," you hand your power to something that doesn't deserve it.

Free your "No."

THE RELATIONAL "NO"

33

Manipulation dies at "No."

I hope you never run into a narcissist, but they are master manipulators. Those caught in the snare of a narcissistic relationship will tell you how many times they wanted to say "No" and instead said yes to things they mentally understood were wrong, outside of their purpose, and even against their intuition and intellect. Still, they said yes. And every time they said yes to the narcissist, they were drawn deeper into the manipulation. Much of the damage caused by manipulators and narcissists can be stopped with a single "No."

Free your "No."

"No" exposes conditional respect.

Are you in a conditional relationship and nobody told you? Do people only deal with you when there are strings attached, conditions on your time, your energy, your resources, all cashed in with your blind yes? And those same people rarely, if ever, return the favor. That's conditional respect. A truly respectful relationship doesn't demand a blank yes check from you. The good news is there's a cure. It's called "No." Take one and call me in the morning.

Free your "No."

Free Your "No."

"No" dismantles delusional obligation.

Who are you really obligated to, and what are you really obligated to do? Isn't it funny how the people we have no legal, moral, or ethical obligation to still expect us to say yes to their requests? They haven't invested in the relationship. They haven't built trust, care, or reciprocity. Yet here you are, afraid to say "No." Afraid to disappoint people who never considered your needs in the first place. Let that sink in, and then free yourself with "No."

Free your "No."

"No" separates partnership from ownership.

In healthy relationships, whether personal or professional, partnership means collaboration, respect, and shared responsibility. But without "No," what began as a partnership can slip into possession where others start to believe they own your time, your talent, and your availability. Ownership demands. Partnership honors. A firm "No" draws the line between the two. It says: You can walk with me, but you cannot walk over me. "No" protects equality in connection and keeps love, work, and service rooted in freedom, not possession.

Free your "No."

"No" prevents you from carrying what was never yours.

Think about how much of what weighs you down doesn't even belong to you. The stress, the obligations, the constant demands … much of it was handed to you, not chosen by you. Yet you keep carrying it, as if saying yes makes you noble, dependable, or worthy. The truth is, it only makes you tired. Your arms are full of responsibilities that were never your life's assignment. Your joy gets lost in tasks that don't serve your purpose.

Free your "No."

"NO" PROTECTS

Silence after "No" is strength.

This busy, loud world of constant stimulation, phones, tablets, computers, and televisions, constantly bombarding us with noise, makes many people afraid of silence. Awkward silence is a powerful technique. However, your "No" isn't awkward; it is power. And it has more power when it's followed by silence, because the receiver of that "No" wants you to create an excuse, possibly a lie. When you give them your unapologetic "No," followed by silence, that silent time becomes a place of renewal and strength in your mind and body, because you exercised the gift of "No."

Free your "No."

"No" is how the strong friend stays the strong friend.

You know why "the strong friend" is "the strong friend"? Oh, you think she's just bold, brilliant, and brave. Do you think she's just naturally able to handle the ebb and flow of life effortlessly because she makes it look easy? Nope. She very well may possess all the attributes you have ascribed to her, but that is not the reason she is the strong friend. She is the strong friend because she has freed her "No." She says it, owns it, exercises it, and honors it.

Free your "No."

Delay makes "No" costlier.

A delayed "No" can be just as costly as a yes. When you hold back your "No," you pay the price in inner turmoil, wrestling with the fact that you wanted to refuse but didn't. The moment you're asked, and you know your answer is "No," is the most powerful, least expensive time to say it. That's when your "No" is clean, quick, and liberated. Once spoken, the shock for the other person is over. After that, everything gets easier. Don't believe me? Try it.

Free your "No."

"No" prevents exploitation.

It doesn't matter if it's your spouse, your supervisor, your children, or your Mama, if yes slides out of your mouth at every request, you will begin to feel exploited. This will not be the fault of the requester. From your lips, the word yes drips too easily. Now you feel subjugated, abused, and exploited because you could not face the possibility of a storm and say "No."

Free your "No."

"No" closes the door to assumption.

Saying yes to everything is like leaving your front door wide open. When you leave your front door open, whether it's for a salesperson, a family member, a friend, or anyone else, whether expected or unexpected, the assumption is that you have time to give them a yes. Learning to exercise a healthy "No" closes the front door, and those who don't have a key must ring the bell and wait to see if you answer. I don't care if they see your car in the driveway. They cannot assume you are available.

Free your "No."

"NO" REDIRECTS

45

"No" is a swift redirection.

If people knew how blessed they are by having that friend, family member, or loved one who tells them "No" immediately and unapologetically, they would rejoice! The requester can now seek their solution, explore the next option, and redirect without wasting any more time. That's a gift.

Free your "No."

"No." protects your dreams.

Do you know what a dreamcatcher is? It's a Native American protective hoop believed to filter dreams, to catch what doesn't belong, nightmares, distractions, and noise while you sleep, so only the good can flow through. That's exactly what your "No" does. Every time you say "No," you're filtering out the confusion, the people-pleasing, the unnecessary burdens that would deplete you. And as the dreamcatcher's feathers guide the good dreams through, your "No" makes room for peace, purpose, and clarity to reach you. "No" is about letting the right things in.

Free your "No."

Free Your "No."

"No" is the root of every authentic yes.

A yes means more, has value, and carries greater meaning when you've exercised your ability to say "No." When you say yes, people feel the worth and the weight of it in a very positive way because they know you know how to say, "No." They know that both they and the thing you said yes to are important and valuable. You're not performing. You're not just obliging. Instead, you are serving and giving from a place of authenticity.

Free your "No."

A clean "No" liberates.

Every human on this earth should be able to experience the liberation and celebration of a clean, crisp, clear, concise "No." Its effects are immediate: Freedom from obligation, clarity of intention, and preservation of energy. It's a jubilant declaration that your time, your purpose, and your peace matter. To say "No" is to step out of bondage and into breath. It is the key that unlocks shackles you didn't even realize were tightening around your life.

Free your "No."

"No" is the compass pointing you back to yourself.

Who, are you? Where are you? Are you doing what you expect to be doing in this season of your life? Do you find yourself busy yet unfulfilled? Are others' requests pulling you outside of yourself and outside of your purpose too often for comfort? Do you feel lost? Do you need direction? When you refuse to say "No," you start veering away from the essence of who you are. "No" is a compass, a guide that uses the earth's magnetic force to pull you back to you.

Free your "No."

"NO" HEALS

51

"NO" HEALS

"No" cures burnout.

Most people don't burn themselves out. Burnout is usually a result of a free-flowing yes to anyone, anything, any project, or request that comes your way. It's in that place that you find yourself burdened and bogged down by things, activities, and responsibilities that don't belong to you. "No" protects your energy and guards your purpose from premature wear and tear. And, it's the key to ending burnout before burnout ends you.

Free your "No."

"No" reduces clutter.

Whether it's physical, mental, emotional, or financial, or spiritual clutter, whatever the clutter, "No" is the reducing agent. Every time you say yes to opportunities and requests without filtering, you're cluttering up your time, your energy, your resources, and your finances with things that don't serve a greater purpose for you, and sometimes even for the requester. If you want to reduce the clutter associated with giving your yes away like it's a party favor, you must learn the discipline of "No."

Free your "No."

"No" quiets chaos.

Say "No" to the next five non-essential, non-life-threatening, non-emergency requests that come your way and watch how beautifully silent and calm your week will become.

Free your "No."

Free Your "No."

"No" reduces back pain.

Literally and figuratively, "No" reduces back pain because you are not out grinding for everyone else. Carrying the weight of other people's expectations bends you, strains you, and wears you down. Constant yeses load your shoulders with responsibilities that were never yours to carry. But when you say "No," you lighten the load. You release the unnecessary grind, the endless hustle, and the pressure to prove yourself through overwork. "No" keeps your back straight, your body strong, and your spirit unburdened. "No" is posture and power in one word. Stand up straight.

Free your "No."

"No" is the prescription for healing.

There is a ton of research that exists that says stress opens the body to disease. So whatever plagues you, if you want to reduce it and its effects on your mental health, physical health, and emotional health, in other words, if you want to begin to heal in any of those areas, there is a cure. The prescription is available to you right now. You don't need a doctor's approval, you don't have to drive to the drug store or order it offline, and it's FREE! Take a few "Nos" and call me in the morning.

Free your "No."

"NO" SURVIVES

57

"No" is necessary.

Your "No" is necessary for balance, necessary for peace, and necessary for freedom. Without it, you will always be pulled in directions that scatter your focus and fracture your strength. Saying "No" is not about withholding love or closing doors. It's about preserving your capacity to show up whole. Your "No" serves as the gatekeeper of your energy, purpose, and health, all of which are essential.

Free your "No."

"No" is survival.

Many people have been conditioned to believe that "No" is selfish. In fact, it can help you survive. "No" as a survival tactic means that nothing and no one is going to put you in harm's way, even up to death. You've seen it in movie plots where a friend says yes to something stupid, and they get involved in something illegal, immoral, or unethical. Or, they are in jail, in danger, or injured. "No" is the way you keep your heart, mind, body, and spirit out of harm's way by not diminishing your health and jeopardizing your life.

Free your "No."

Your "NO" is self-care.

Forget the spa, the massage, the nails done, and the haircut - and all that! Forget the candles, forget the incense, forget the bubble bath. Forget the shopping spree. The highest expression of self-care is found in your ability to exercise your "No."

Free your "No."

"No" is the currency of freedom.

Time is freedom. Many people want more time, but they can't say "No." You have freedom, where do you spend it? Your time is wrapped up in too many yesses. If you want to start that hobby, take that trip, write that book, paint that picture, then you must stop saying yes to everyone and everything! You're spending your currency on every yes you give to something that isn't in alignment with your purpose, doesn't bring you joy, or doesn't edify something or someone in any way.

Free your "No."

Free Your "No."

"No" is debt-free.

When you say "No," you free up your time, your energy, your joy, your love, and your resources. "No" carries no debt. A clear and immediate "No" means you owe nothing else, no excuses, no guilt, no lingering obligations. Your "No" releases you to invest your resources where they matter most – in your peace, in serving your community, in loving your family, and in breathing. Yes, just the ability to inhale and exhale. "No" doesn't come with debt; it leaves you free.

Free your "No."

"NO" IS STRATEGIC

63

Free Your "NO"

"No" is a strategy.

Saying "No" to a third donut, saying "No" to illicit drugs and excessive alcohol, and saying "No" to a party is a strategy for healthy living. And, that's the same reason saying "No" to carrying someone else's burden, to pushing yourself beyond healthy physical limits, and allowing yourself to take part in things that diminish your logic and livelihood is a strategy. Saying "No" is a strategy for building, designing, and creating a healthy and balanced life.

Free your "No."

"No" breeds brilliance.

Brilliance requires clarity, and clarity cannot exist in the clutter of unnecessary yeses. Your brilliance cannot shine with cloudy vision and scattered energy. Every intentional "No" clears space for focus, creativity, and innovation. Brilliance is not born from BUSY-ness; it emerges from boundaries. It is the pruning that produces growth, the silence that sparks ideas, the discipline that sharpens genius. "No" amplifies brilliance.

Free your "No."

"No" clears your calendar.

A packed schedule is not proof of importance. It's often evidence of misplaced priorities. BUSY-ness looks impressive, but is it really? When you say "No," you create space for what matters most. A "No" on your calendar is not a blank space. It's a boundary. "No" is not an empty slot on your to-do list; it's a power move. It's a statement that your time is valuable enough to be filled with a "No" instead of being occupied by everyone else's demands. "No" makes room for intention, not occupancy.

Free your "No."

"No" resists bargaining.

A "No" does not negotiate, compromise, or twist itself into a softer version to make others comfortable. A true "No" is final and doesn't come with conditions, concessions, or loopholes. When you mean "No," you don't owe a trade-off to ease the sting. Bargaining weakens your boundary, but a firm "No" strengthens it. Saying "No" with conviction communicates clarity: I know my limits, I know my priorities, and I refuse to put them up for sale or on clearance.

Free your "No."

"No" attracts authenticity.

Every time you say "No," you draw in people who value honesty, respect boundaries, and see your worth beyond what you can provide. "No" attracts opportunities that align with your purpose and that match your capacity. It beckons clarity, truth, and relationships rooted in respect. When you practice "No," you send out a signal, a beacon, and only what is real, and only what is aligned. Only what honors you is answered. And that's the power. "No" attracts what's genuine.

Free your "No."

"NO" IS HUMANE

69

"No" values humanity, not productivity.

In a world that measures worth by output, "No" reminds us that people are not machines. You are not defined by how much you grind, how many boxes you check, or how many hours you give away. "No" says your rest matters, your health matters, and your soul matters. It prioritizes dignity and well-being over production. Productivity is about quotas, but humanity is about life. Every "No" is a declaration that you are more than what you produce; you are worthy simply by being.

Free your "No."

Free Your "No."

"No" breaks generational curses disguised as duty.

Too many families pass down exhaustion as love, silence as respect, and self-denial as responsibility. Generations have worn themselves out under the weight of obligation, calling it honor, when in truth it is bondage. "No" is the word that interrupts the cycle. It says, "I can love you without losing me." You can honor the past without carrying its bondage. Duty rooted in sacrifice without boundaries is not a legacy. A clear "No" sets you free and shifts the trajectory of the inheritance you leave on this earth.

Free your "No."

Free Your "No."

Without "No," loyalty becomes a leash.

What should be a bond of trust turns into a chain of control, dragging you where you don't belong. You are not a dog. Loyalty without boundaries is domination. When every request demands a yes, somebody is mistaking faithfulness for obedience. True loyalty thrives with balance, where your "No" garners the same respect as your yes. A firm "No" keeps loyalty voluntary, and that's the only way it's pure. Otherwise, the leash tightens until loyalty is no longer love – it's a type of captivity.

Free your "No."

"No" ensures your needs aren't erased in theirs.

When you always say yes, your priorities fade into the background while others dominate the stage. Over time, your voice grows quieter, your desires smaller, until your life is written in someone else's handwriting. That is the danger of erasure. You become actively absent. A clear "No" stops the overwrite. It protects your space in the story and your right to exist fully as much as anyone else.

Free your "No."

"No" keeps compassion from becoming captivity.

Your kindness can turn into a cage where people mistake your giving for their entitlement. Compassion is powerful when it flows freely, but it becomes dangerous when it's demanded. Saying "No" does not diminish your love, your care, or your willingness to serve. It protects it. "No" sets the boundaries that keep compassion pure, healthy, and sustainable. It ensures you are giving from choice, not compulsion, and that your freedom remains intact even while you love deeply.

Free your "No."

"NO" FORECASTS

75

Free Your
"NO"

"No" is a predictor of your future.

What you say "No" to now will open the door to the yes you want later. What you say "No" to now creates space for the yeses that build your future. Every refusal is a seed planted for tomorrow. Saying "No" is about positioning. It's a declaration that you want a future built with purpose, by purpose, on purpose, and for purpose! Your "No" today makes room for the yes your destiny requires.

Free your "No."

Free Your "No."

"No" keeps you chosen.

You're rare. You're one out of eight billion people on the earth. Every time you say "No," you protect what makes you unique. You are not common, not replaceable, and certainly not for everyone's convenience. The world will try to treat you as ordinary, but "No" reminds them you are set apart. To be chosen means you are selected. "No" preserves you to accomplish the unique and specific things assigned to you on earth.

Free your "No."

"No" unlocks your now.

Every beginning requires an ending, and every beginning requires space. When you keep saying yes to today's requests, tomorrow gets farther away, and tomorrow does not have the room to grow. A "No" today is about being present enough to know tomorrow needs you. "No" means you're not now-focused. You're next-focused. Your next opportunity, your next level, your next chapter is waiting on your willingness to say "No."

Free your "No."

Free Your "No."

"No" today shapes tomorrow.

Every "No" is like the hands of a potter as the clay revolves, giving it meaning, shape, and texture. The potter says, "No" to granules or flecks in the clay, so the shaping process is smoother. "No" defines the edges of your future, giving form to your priorities and substance to your vision. It may not feel easy in the moment, but it protects your time and opens the way for growth, rest, and direction. The future you want is not built by saying yes to everything. It is built because you shape it. Every "No" you give today is a decision that influences the shape of your life tomorrow.

Free your "No."

"No" preserves capacity.

Capacity is your ability to think clearly, love fully, and work effectively without being stretched past your limits. Every unnecessary yes eats away at that capacity, leaving you overloaded and unable to give your best where it matters most. But "No" protects your bandwidth. It guards your time, energy, and mental space, allowing you to stay sharp, present, and effective. "No" is not about withholding. It's about reserving enough strength to pour into the right people, the right priorities, and the right purpose. "No" ensures you have the capacity to hold the future before you.

Free your "No."

"NO" GROWS AND ABOUNDS

82

Free Your
"NO"

"NO" GROWS AND ABOUNDS

"No" multiplies energy.

Every careless yes drains your strength, scattering it in too many directions. But every intentional "No" gathers your energy, focuses it, and makes it stronger. What feels like holding back is really building up. "No" keeps you from pouring into what depletes you, so you have more to give where it matters. It's not subtraction. It's multiplication. Each "No" preserves power, protects focus, and produces the momentum you need to move farther, faster, and with far more impact.

Free your "No."

"No" creates room for overflow.

Overflow doesn't happen when your life is packed to the brim with obligations, distractions, and constant demands. That's not overflow – that's overload. Overflow is the result of space, margin, and intentional focus. Every "No" you speak clears the clutter that keeps you stretched thin and opens capacity for more of what nourishes you. "No" makes room for creativity to flow, for peace to settle, for joy to rise, and for abundance to spill over into every part of your life. Then your overflow extends to the ones you love, organizations you serve, and all of humanity.

Free your "No."

"No" keeps you from being wasteful.

Waste is using valuable resources, time, energy, money, or even love on things that bring no return and create no growth. "No" keeps you from being wasteful. Every careless yes pours what is precious into places that cannot hold it, draining you without replenishment. Waste occurs when you spread yourself across commitments that don't align with your purpose. But "No" protects what matters. It redirects your effort into fertile ground where it can multiply. With "No," your resources are not squandered. They are preserved and positioned for greater impact.

Free your "No."

"No" is wealth.

Every time you say "No," you're saving your most valuable resources – your time, your energy, and your focus. Wealth isn't only about money; it's about stewardship. A careless yes squanders you, leaving you broke in spirit and bankrupt in peace. But "No" is an investment. It keeps your account full so you can give with intention, not out of obligation. "No" grows interest in your future, multiplies your capacity, and preserves what matters most. That's real wealth – living fully and not drained.

Free your "No."

"No" keeps you from pouring into bottomless pits.

Both leeches and pits are takers, but they take in different ways. A leech attaches itself to you and drains until it is full, then it detaches, only to return when it's hungry again. A pit, on the other hand, has no end. No matter how much you pour in, time, love, energy, or money – it never fills, never satisfies, and never gives back. Saying yes to takers keeps you depleted. "No" preserves your strength for places where your pouring produces fruit.

Free your "No."

"NO" BUILDS ROOTS

Free Your "NO"

"NO" BUILDS ROOTS

"No" is fertilizer.

The purpose of fertilizer is not to look pretty on the surface. It goes deep, breaks down, and enriches the soil beneath the surface so something beautiful can grow. Fertilizer smells strong, feels messy, and often looks like (or is) waste, but it produces nourishment that leads to harvest and bounty, just like your "No." Your "No" might feel uncomfortable in the moment, but it is feeding your future. Every "No" enriches your boundaries, strengthens your roots, and prepares the ground for the fruit you are meant to bear.

Free your "No."

"No" establishes roots.

Roots must go down before they can grow up. They dig deep into the soil, anchoring, stabilizing, and drawing strength long before anything is visible above ground. In the same way, your "No" is about depth – the kind of depth that produces wisdom, focus, and discipline. Shallow living comes from saying yes to everything. Deep living comes from saying "No." It grows the unseen foundation that allows you to build a valuable life on a firm foundation.

Free your "No."

"No" protects planted seeds.

Every idea, dream, or goal you carry starts fragile. If you say "Yes" to everything, you risk exposing it, trampling it, or starving it. "No" is the shield that guards your investment until it's strong enough to grow. It's the fence that keeps out what doesn't belong. Without "No," your seeds don't stand a chance of becoming fruit.

Free your "No."

"No" protects the harvest.

Planting seeds is only the beginning. The true reward comes when the fruit is ready to be plucked and enjoyed. Without "No," your harvest is at risk, taken too soon, trampled by others, or wasted on those who never sowed with you. Yes to everything leaves your field exposed, but "No" guards the fruit until it's ripe, ready, and yours to have. A clear "No" ensures that what you've grown can be gathered in season and used with purpose.

Free your "No."

"No" grounds you.

Grounding, as a spiritual practice, is the intentional act of connecting yourself to the present moment, to the Earth, and to the source that steadies you. It is about becoming rooted mind, body, and spirit so you are not carried away by chaos or consumed by distraction. In the same way, "No" grounds you. Each time you say it, you anchor yourself back to truth. You stand firm in who you are instead of being swayed by every request.

Free your "No."

"NO" IS AN ADULT

"No" is maturity.

Saying "No" is one of the most grown-up, responsible, and self-aware things you can ever do. Immaturity says yes to be liked, to avoid conflict, or to keep the peace at the expense of oneself. Maturity recognizes that unchecked yeses lack maturity. Grow up and say "No."

Your discerning "No" indicates your discipline is mature, your decision-making is mature, and your ability to enforce your boundaries is mature.

To say "No" is to stand firm in who you are and steward your life like an adult.

Free your "No."

Free Your "No."

"No" develops wisdom.

Wisdom is not just knowing what to do. It is knowing what *not* to do. Every time you say "No," you practice discernment. Wisdom grows in the pauses, in the boundaries, in the refusals that keep you aligned with your purpose. A careless yes is not wisdom. "No" clears it. Over time, those choices shape a wise life, one guided by clarity and grounded in truth.

Free your "No."

"No" builds resilience.

Every time you say "No," you strengthen your ability to withstand pressure, resist manipulation, and rise above the weight of other people's expectations. Resilience isn't formed in constant agreement. It's forged in boundaries. "No" teaches you to endure being misunderstood, to stand firm when others push back, and to stay rooted when guilt tries to sway you. Over time, you don't just bounce back; you stand taller, stronger, and unshaken.

Free your "No."

"No" rebuilds strength.

Strength is not rebuilt by doing more but by protecting your reserves and choosing where you place your effort. Each time you say "No," you stop the unnecessary drain and begin to restore what was lost. It allows your body to rest, your mind to reset, and your spirit to recover. "No" is the strategy that rebuilds your power.

Free your "No."

"No" builds confidence.

Every time you say it with clarity, you prove to yourself that you can stand firm in your decisions. Confidence is not just about speaking up. It's about backing yourself even when others oppose you. Over time, the fear of disappointing others fades, and the assurance of honoring yourself grows. Saying "No" becomes a declaration of confidence, strength, and self-trust. Confidence turns hesitation into action, fear into courage, silence into voice, and uncertainty into a clear path forward.

Free your "No."

THE CLARITY OF "NO"

Free Your "NO"

"No" prevents control masquerading as love.

What if I told you that you could love someone and not yield to their every request? What if I told you that you should sift through and accept requests that are made of you, even when made by someone you love? Without "No" love becomes control. Repeat after me:

I can love you and not give in.

I can love you and be unavailable.

I can love you and need space.

I can love you and say "No," because love is not control. It's freedom.

Free your "No."

"No" stops strength from being mistaken for servitude.

Too often, capable people are drained because others confuse their willingness with weakness or their power with permission. Strength is a gift, but it is not an endless well for everyone else's demands. When you refuse to say "No," you risk becoming confined by the very people you intended to help. Saying "No" reclaims your authority. It draws the line that protects your strength, honors your boundaries, and reminds the world that your service is a choice, not an obligation.

Free your "No."

"No" anchors you.

Just like a boat drifting without an anchor is at the mercy of the waves, a life without boundaries is tossed in every direction. Saying yes to everything leaves you unstable and pulled by currents that take you out into the deep blue sea. But "No" drops the anchor. It secures you in place, keeping you steady when demands and expectations try to push you off course. With "No," you are not lost at sea. You are stable, balanced, and firmly aligned with your purpose.

Free your "No."

Yes, without "No" blinds you.

When you keep saying yes without discrimination, you lose sight of yourself, your needs, and your joy. Your vision becomes clouded by everyone else's demands, obscuring your own path, priorities, and purpose. A life of constant yeses feels busy, but so unfocused, as if you're navigating through the fog of your life. "No" clears the fog. It restores clarity, sharpens vision, and opens your eyes to what truly matters. With "No," your yes becomes a choice rooted in 20/20 vision.

Free your "No."

"No" revives.

To revive means to bring back to life, to restore strength, energy, or consciousness. Revival is about renewal, breathing fresh life into what was fading. That is what "No" does. When life leaves you drained from endless yeses, a firm "No" restores you. It gives your body rest, your mind clarity, and your spirit room to breathe again. Each time you say it, you are revived, renewed, and reconnected to the best version of yourself.

Free your "No."

"NO" BINDS AND SECURES

Free Your "NO"

The easiest "No" is a now "No."

Delayed refusals turn into complicated explanations, awkward excuses, and crushing guilt you never needed to carry. A quick "No" is clean. It's direct. It's final. It saves you from the weight of overthinking and the resentment of overcommitting. The longer you wait to say it, the harder it becomes, and the more tangled the situation gets. A now "No" preserves your peace, clarity, and credibility. The easiest limit to define is the one you set immediately.

Free your "No."

Boundaries begin at "No."

I have been taught to guard my heart because - everything I do flows from my heart. In simple terms, that means I have to protect my inner peace, my emotions, and my thoughts, because they shape the way I live, love, and lead; how I show up in life. Guarding your heart is about setting boundaries, paying attention to what you allow in, and being intentional about what you release out. You cannot set, enforce, and protect a boundary without exercising "No."

Free your "No."

"No" evicts leeches.

There is no such thing as a generous leech. A leech has one assignment: To suck until it's full. In fact, it can take up to five times its own body weight in blood before it finally detaches to digest. People can act the same way, feeding off your love, peace, joy, finances, and energy until they're overflowing. Then, when they've burned through it, they circle back for more. If you don't set boundaries, they'll keep draining you. Remember this: Leeches don't give, they only take. Protect your life. Protect your purpose. Say "No" to leeches.

Free your "No."

"No" is the firewall against emotional theft.

A firewall protects your computer by blocking harmful intrusions, filtering what comes into your computer, and keeping valuable data safe. In the same way, "No" protects your heart and mind. It stops unwanted demands from slipping in, filters out distractions, and safeguards your emotional resources from being stolen. Without a firewall, your system is wide open to viruses. Without "No," your spirit is wide open to depletion. Saying "No" secures your purpose from being hacked.

Free your "No."

Free Your "No."

"No" ends scarcity.

Scarcity arises from overextending and pouring into everything and everyone, until you believe there's never enough time, energy, or even enough of yourself. Did I say money? Money too. When you always say yes, you feed the scarcity mindset, chasing every demand as if it's your only chance. But "No" changes the flow. "No" stops the fear of missing out (FOMO). Now, instead of living in lack, you live in abundance. Your time, creativity, love, and joy expand because you no longer see your life as lacking.

Free your "No."

"NO" DISCERNS

Free Your "NO"

"No" makes room for a quality "Yes."

Quantity says yes to everything, chasing approval and scattering your energy across too much. Quality understands that fewer, intentional yeses create more impact than a pile of shallow ones. When you practice "No," you eliminate the noise and protect your capacity. What is left is stronger, sharper, and more meaningful. A quality yes carries weight because it is rare and deliberate. Saying "No" ensures your agreement is not cheap or common but valuable and powerful.

Free your "No."

"No" attracts the right yes.

Saying "No" attracts the right yes. Every refusal clears the clutter of obligations that don't belong to you. Each time you say "No," you create space for alignment, for the opportunities that complement your purpose. A scattered yes invites confusion, but a strategic "No" invites clarity. The right yes doesn't compete with your peace, it complements it. It doesn't drain you. It develops you. Saying "No" is not about closing doors. It is about making sure the right doors can open.

Free your "No."

"No" is a secure password.

A password protects access, keeps intruders out, and ensures that only what is authorized can get through. In the same way, "No" guards your time, energy, and peace. Without it, anyone can log into your life, drain your resources, and override your priorities. A strong password is not easy to guess, and a strong "No" is not easy to push past. Saying it locks out what does not belong and secures what matters most to you.

Free your "No."

"No" resists idolatry.

Idolatry happens when people, positions, or possessions are worshipped. When you cannot say "No," you risk elevating others' approval, their needs, or their demands above your own. A constant yes bows to pressure, but "No" stands in reverence to what is higher, purer, and more accurate. Saying "No" reminds you that nothing and no one deserves idolization. "No" keeps your worship off anything that doesn't serve, and it protects what's sacred in and to you.

Free your "No."

"NO" IS CAPTIVATING

"No" is magnetic.

It draws the right people, opportunities, and energy toward you while repelling what doesn't belong. Saying "No" signals strength and self-awareness, and that kind of confidence is naturally attractive. People respect and are drawn to someone who guards their time and values. "No" doesn't push everything away; it pulls the right things closer.

Free your "No."

"No" is seductive."

The word "No" has an irresistible quality: It commands attention, sparks curiosity, and pulls the right things toward you. It intrigues because it isn't freely given. A clear "No" shows restraint, discipline, and power, and that makes people lean in. What we can't easily have becomes more desirable. "No" commands attention, sets the standard, and leaves space for curiosity. That's the quiet allure of "No." It lures without chasing.

Free your "No."

"No" is bold.

It takes courage to stand firm when saying yes would be easier. "No" challenges expectations and disrupts the patterns of people-pleasing. It refuses to shrink back or hide behind excuses. Boldness is not about being loud. It's about being clear, direct, and unshakable. Each "No" declares, *I know who I am, I know what I want, and I refuse to settle for less.* "No" dares to protect your truth, and that's attractive.

Free your "No."

"No" is irresistible.

Irresistible means impossible to ignore or deny, and that's exactly what "No" becomes when spoken with conviction. In a world overflowing with constant yeses, a firm "No stands out. It signals confidence, clarity, and conviction, qualities that naturally draw people in. "No" doesn't beg for approval; it commands respect. It leaves people curious, challenged, and sometimes inspired. "No" is irresistible because it shows that you will not be owned by demands but guided by purpose.

Free your "No."

"No" is unapologetic.

Unapologetic means free from regret, unafraid of judgment, and unwilling to trade truth for approval. It doesn't stumble over explanations or shrink under pressure. It stands tall without the need to justify itself. It pulls people in because it radiates confidence and certainty. Every unapologetic "No" is an act of self-respect. It affirms your beliefs, establishes clear boundaries around what you will and will not allow, and strengthens the foundation of your identity. "No" is unapologetic because it declares your right to choose without excuse or apology.

Free your "No."

THE JOY OF "NO"

Free Your "No."

"Yes" is the thief of joy.

Sure, you've heard the phrase *comparison is the thief of joy,* and that's true. But just like comparison, yes can rob your joy blind. Every time you say yes to what isn't aligned with your purpose, you're saying no to your well-being, your focus, and your strength. When you agree to something outside your purpose, you sacrifice your goals, your direction, and your influence. Whether you put comparison first or yes first, the result is the same – stolen joy.

Free your "No."

"No" makes joy possible.

Joy does not live on the surface. It rests deep inside, where peace, freedom, and wholeness breathe together. When you surrender to every demand, joy is pushed into hiding, suffocated beneath weight that does not belong to you. But "No" lifts the heaviness. It makes room for your spirit to exhale and for your soul to remember itself. Joy is not created by activity, but by space. Every "No" becomes an opening, a clearing, where joy can finally rise, unashamed and uncontained, to take its rightful place within you.

Free your "No."

"No" creates joy.

True joy is not an accident. It is crafted in the silence, in the courage to choose what nourishes you and release what diminishes you. Joy is not born from excess but from intention. Saying "No" is how you write joy into your own story. It is how you carve out space for what makes your spirit sing. Joy is not about doing more. It is about becoming more free, more present, more whole. "No" is the chisel, and joy is the sculpture revealed when the excess is cut away.

Free your "No."

"No" is the defender of your joy.

Joy is delicate and powerful all at once. But without protection, it can be stolen by demands, drained by performance, and silenced by guilt. "No" stands guard at the doorway of your soul, refusing entry to what seeks to rob you. It shields your inner light from being dimmed, your laughter from being muted, and your peace from being disturbed. Joy cannot survive unguarded. It thrives when "No" is present, vigilant, and unwavering. In every refusal, you preserve joy's sanctuary within, safe, whole, and eternally yours.

Free your "No."

"No" sustains joy.

Every time you choose "No" over obligation, commitment, or distraction, you choose to protect what truly matters. "No" is not rejection; it's preservation. It keeps your energy from being scattered, your focus from being divided, and your heart from being drained. By saying "No," you honor your limits and create space for what brings genuine fulfillment. Joy doesn't thrive in BUSY-ness or in pleasing everyone else. It flourishes when you guard it with intentional boundaries. In this way, "No" is not a loss but a gift that sustains your joy for the long journey ahead.

Free your "No."

CONCLUSION

129

Free Your **"NO"**

Free Your "No."

Now you "No."

So here you are, at the end of this journey, yet really, you are standing at the beginning of owning your "No." You now know the truth: a life without "No" leaves you drained, resentful, and disconnected from yourself. But a life anchored in "No" creates space for joy, wholeness, and even self-actualization.

The question is no longer *if* you will say "No," but *how* you will choose to say it, when to honor it, and what kind of life you will build because of it. Saying "No" is about direction. It points you back to what matters most, aligns you with your values, and opens the door to your truest yes.

Free Your "No."

"No" is not a wall; it is a door. A door that leads to clarity, peace, and purpose. It is both shield and guide, protecting your energy and pointing you toward freedom.

Let this be the moment you shift from permission to power. May your "No" make every yes sacred, intentional, and free. Because in the end, saying "No" is not the end at all, it's the beginning of building, creating, and orchestrating the life you were always meant to live.

May you walk with courage to declare it, the strength to sustain it, and the faith to trust what lies beyond it. Let "No" be your covenant with yourself. May it lead you into the abundant life that has always awaited you.

May "No" open space for happiness, for healing, for the presence of love in your daily steps. May the sacred strength of "No" silence what drains you. Each "No" is a prayer of alignment. Step boldly into the life ordained for you, where clarity reigns and peace abides.

May you carry the sacred power of "No" as both shield and song. Let every "No" you speak consecrate your yes making it pure, purposeful, and free. Go forward in courage, knowing that "No" is not denial, it is divine direction. And it will lead you home to yourself.

The more you *"No."*

Saying "No" often carries mixed emotions, relief and guilt, freedom and fear, strength and trembling. That is the sacred tension of boundaries. Yet with each "No," the fog begins to lift. You realize you are not closing doors; you are clearing pathways. You are not rejecting others; you are protecting yourself.

Saying "No" is rarely simple. At first, it may sit heavy in your chest, leaving you uneasy or second-guessing yourself. You may worry about disappointing others, being misunderstood, or missing out. The weight of obligation can make yes feel safer, even when it costs you peace

Free Your "No."

Over time, the sting of saying "No" softens, replaced by the steady assurance that you are living with integrity. And in that clarity, your yes regains its power. It becomes intentional, rooted, and free.

So let your "No" shake you at first if it must, but don't let it break you or deter you from exercising it. The mixed emotions fade, but the clarity remains. And clarity is where joy, peace, and purpose begin.

Free Your "No."

Wouldn't you love to "No"

No is a love language. It is how we tell ourselves; *I matter.* You're refusing to stretch yourself thin, refusing to betray your own values for the comfort of others.

Boundaries set by freeing your "No" are not barriers; they are bridges to healthier relationships, stronger commitments, and truer connections. Every time you free your "No," you create room for laughter, rest, creativity, and the things that make life meaningful.

"No" honors the limited time you've been given on this earth. Each "No" is a declaration that your days are too precious to be wasted. And here is the truth: every "No" you speak today swings open a door of love tomorrow—love for yourself, love for the right people, love for the work that matters, and love for the life you are called to live.

"No" opens the door to love of self, the kind that refuses to sacrifice your well-being for temporary approval.

The power of "No" is this: it reveals love that is mutual, not one-sided. It brings love that sees your worth clearly and discards anything that doesn't. And ultimately, no opens the door to love that lasts because it is rooted in truth, not performance.

"No" How

How do you say "No?"

1.   Pause Before You Answer

Give yourself permission not to respond immediately. Silence is powerful. A pause allows space to check in with your heart before your mouth commits.

2. Check Alignment

Ask: Does this request honor my values, energy, and priorities? If the answer is no, then your answer must be "No."

3. Start Small

Practice "No" in low-stakes situations—declining extra commitments, unnecessary purchases, or unwanted invitations. Build confidence one boundary at a time.

4. Use Compassionate Clarity

You don't need long explanations. A simple, kind, and firm "No" is enough. Respect your words by keeping them short and steady.

5. Replace Guilt With Gratitude

Instead of feeling guilty for saying "No," thank yourself for protecting your peace and creating room for what matters most.

6. Celebrate Your Wins

Each time you say "No," acknowledge the freedom it created. Let those small victories strengthen your courage for the bigger ones.

7. Create a "Yes" List

Write down the people, priorities, and passions that deserve your "Yes." Let this list guide you so every "No" protects what matters most.

8. Enlist Accountability

Share your commitment to saying "No" with a trusted friend, coach, or mentor. Let them remind you when old habits try to creep back in.

9. Anchor in the Sacred

Treat "No" as a spiritual practice. Journal about how saying "No" draws you closer to peace, purpose, and God's design for your life.

10. Commit to the Journey

Remember: "No" is not a one-time act but a lifestyle shift. Keep practicing until it becomes your natural, sacred rhythm.

"No" it all

Remember, when you Free Your "No" it is not meant to harden your heart or keep you from opportunity or responsibility. If every answer becomes "No," you may find yourself just as bound as when you never said it at all.

The danger is moving from people-pleasing to self-protecting so fiercely that you shut out the very joy you seek, connection, and growth. "No" was never meant to become your shield against all of life, it was meant to be your filter.

A wise "No" allows you to discern which invitations align with your values, which relationships nurture your soul, and which responsibilities honor your purpose. Saying "Yes" to what is right, whole, and life-giving is just as essential as refusing what is draining.

The yes/no balance is where peace lives. It creates the discernment where clarity thrives. And it's there, where the courage is found in choosing both the "No" that protects and the yes that propels.

Your job is to learn the rhythm, when to close the door and when to open the door, when to say yes and when to Free Your "No."

ABOUT THE AUTHOR

**"I lead individuals and organizations
from Elusive to Empowered."**

Dr. Timogi is a Corporate Trainer and Keynote Speaker with experience in corporate, nonprofit, and higher education leadership. She is the founder of Create & Facilitate, a North Carolina HUB Certified Customized Training Solutions Agency, specializing in training programs, Executive Coaching, and employee mediation. As an international keynote speaker, Dr. Timogi has inspired and trained diverse audiences, ranging from correctional facilities to prestigious institutions like Harvard. She is also the author of 17 books and numerous customized training programs, demonstrating her commitment to empowering individuals and organizations worldwide.

www.DrTimogi.com
www.CreateAndFacilitate.com

Free Your "No."

Book Dr. Timogi Today!

Leadership Training and Development

Keynote Speeches

Panel Discussions and Panel Moderator

Executive Coaching

Individual and Group Coaching

Conferences

Employee Training and Development

Commencements

Workplace Conflict Mediation

Retreats

Customized Certifications

CONTACT INFORMATION

PO Box 334
Lexington, NC 27293
www.DrTimogi.com
DrTimogi@CreateAndFAcilitate.com
www.CreateAndFacilitate.com